100

THINGS TO DO IN
CHARLOTTESVILLE
BEFORE YOU
DIE

100

THINGS TO DO IN CHARLOTTESVILLE BEFORE YOU DIE

• •

MARIJEAN OLDHAM

REEDY PRESS

Library of Congress Control Number: 2018940102

ISBN: 9781681061580

Design by Jill Halpin

Printed in the United States of America
18 19 20 21 22   5 4 3 2 1

Please note that websites, phone numbers, addresses, and company names are subject to change or cancellation. We did our best to relay the most accurate information available, but due to circumstances beyond our control, please do not hold us liable for misinformation. When exploring new destinations, please do your homework before you go.

To Seth,

I'm so lucky to have you by my side.

CONTENTS

Music and Entertainment

Sports and Recreation

Culture and History

• •

• •

PREFACE

I fell hard for Charlottesville shortly after moving here at the end of 2005. Many others report the same kind of C'ville love, and in fact, people who first came to town as University of Virginia students often feel the call to return post-graduation. Central Virginia has a lot going for it that I like: wine, beautiful outdoor adventures, great food, smart people, social consciousness, and a lively arts scene. Charlottesville may be small, but it fits my personality like a glove.

The place that won me over on my first visit was the central highlight of the city: the Downtown Mall. No visit to Charlottesville is complete without a stroll on the pedestrian mall, a peek into the shops, a bite to eat at an outdoor restaurant, people watching, and busker-driven entertainment.

If the Downtown Mall is the center of Charlottesville, I think the radius extends for special occasions to nearby Staunton, Va. where the American Shakespeare Center has its home, to Shenandoah National Park for hiking and camping adventures, up north to Kegler's Lanes for a bowling date, or down south to the James River for a summertime tubing day. Part of the fun of this town is what's easily accessible, so get out and enjoy it!

Writing this book began as a relatively easy exercise; ideas of what to do based on what I've done and what I hope to do just flowed onto the page. The challenge, of course, was whittling down to 100, and trying to fit the best of what's here on these pages. A formidable task to be sure. Each recommendation was carefully considered and often personally investigated. The ideas keep coming, however, and with every season it seems new and exciting things to do are available in this historic village. Plan a visit, soon, and if you're a townie, get to work on crossing off your list of *100 Things to Do in Charlottesville Before You Die*.

• •

ACKNOWLEDGMENTS

This is not the kind of book meant to be written, read, or experienced alone. A great many thanks go out to my six million (according to my dad) Facebook friends who shouted out great ideas. I've heard from folks intending to launch clubs designed to check off each recommended activity, and I'm eager to hear from those who do. Special thanks to Seth Oldham, my sweetie and the cyclist who told me about the best route in the region. Thank you to my daughter, Allison Jaggers, whose late night brainstorming sessions helped make sure nothing was left out. Thank you to my son, Aaron Jaggers, for enthusiasm and a general sense of joy surrounding this project. Mountains of appreciation for Mary Sproles Martin who keeps my hyphenating to a minimum and my capitalization in order, and last but not least, thank you to Amanda Doyle who thought of me and of Charlottesville.

FOOD AND DRINK

MAKE A CHEESE PILGRIMAGE
TO THE MONASTERY IN WHITE HALL

Trust me on this: go to White Hall and buy some Gouda cheese handmade by the nuns. The neighboring rural community of White Hall has only a couple of things going for it, but oh, are they worth it. First is a Trappist monastery, Our Lady of the Angels, populated and managed by a group of monastic nuns who, when they're not praying for our souls, make the most delicious cheese! Bring cash—a wheel of Gouda is $25 and worth every penny, and the scenic journey to get it.

If you like a little wine with your cheese, you're in luck. Pack some fruit, bread, and crackers to go with your cheese and head to White Hall Winery for a perfect fall afternoon with friends.

Our Lady of the Angels Monastery
3365 Monastery Dr., Crozet 22932-2116
434-823-1452
www.olamonastery.org

White Hall Vineyards
5282 Sugar Ridge Rd., Crozet 22932
434-823-8615
www.whitehallvineyards.com

PICK YOUR OWN FRUIT
FROM AN ORCHARD

We recommend peaches and strawberries from Chile's Orchard in Crozet in the summer, and apples from Carter Mountain Orchard in the fall. Plan the trip to either orchard as an outing with the kids. Carter Mountain can be a long trip up the mountain in peak season with lots of other apple-pickers, and conditions can be quite muddy. Step out of the orchard and into the Prince Michel Vineyard and Winery tasting room on the premises, or stock up on apple butter, baked goods, crafts, and recipe books in the gift shop.

A visit to Chile's is a bit more straightforward with a peach's time from tree to cashier to your car at a minimum, but stick around for a while and sample the fresh peach frozen custard before you head home to make your pies and cobblers.

Chiles Peach Orchard
1351 Greenwood Rd., Crozet 22932
434-823-1583
www.chilespeachorchard.com

Carter Mountain Orchard
1435 Carters Mountain Trail, Charlottesville 22901
434-977-1833
www.cartermountainorchard.com

EAT LIKE A EUROPEAN
WITH A CRÊPE FROM THE FLAT

Get a crêpe from the Flat and stroll the mall listening to buskers play guitar, harmonica, or both while you munch away on the French-inspired cuisine in a paper wrapper. The Flat is a tiny, almost invisible takeaway crêperie on Water Street, just off the Downtown Mall. The building is Lilliputian and the kitchen is a half-story below street level, as you'll see when you step up to the window to place your order. Try the Epic Veg and the Nutella and Banana crêpes, but any crêpe will do quite nicely. The Flat is closed on Mondays, so save your cravings for another day.

11 Water St. E., 434-978-3528

MEET YOUR EATS
AT LOCAL FARMS

The Meet Yer Eats Farm Tour has grown steadily in popularity since its inception. A Labor Day Weekend exclusive, Market Central, which manages the weekly seasonal City Market downtown, takes people to the farms that supply our city's farmers' markets. Get a car pass and visit a selection of a dozen or more participating farms to see exactly where the area's produce, meats, and dairy come from, and meet the farmers responsible for supplying us with fresh foods nearby. During the rest of the year, when you see a local provider listed on a restaurant menu, or see their foods available at any of our markets, you'll have your own story to tell about the day you met the people who provide that food to our community.

Market Central Inc.
P.O. Box 201
www.marketcentralonline.org
meetyereats.wordpress.com

BE A NACHOVORE
ALL OVER TOWN

Before you die, you need to make multiple trips to Beer Run. One trip should be with a small group and include tasting several craft beers and consuming your weight in nachos. The nachos at Beer Run are my favorite nachos in the world.

Another trip should be for brunch on a Sunday. Include the best Bloody Mary with your meal, if you're so inclined, or perhaps a mimosa if you have a sweet tooth. The food is fantastic. They open at 11 a.m. and, no matter the time of year, are packed to the gills in short order, so get there early or, at worst, right on time. The third trip you make to Beer Run should be reflective. Sit at the bar and talk to the locals. Meet Bill. Browse the selection of beer-to-go and take some with you. You'll recall the visits fondly no matter how long it is between your last visit and your next.

OTHER GREAT NACHOS

Beer Run

156 Carlton Rd. #203, Charlottesville 22902
434-984-2337
www.beerrun.com

Mono Loco

200 Water St. W, Charlottesville 22902
434-979-0688
www.monolocorestaurant.com

Continental Divide

811 W. Main St., Charlottesville 22903
434-984-0143

LEARN TO COOK

Take a cooking class at the Charlottesville Cooking School—sample everything from Indian cooking to holiday pie workshops, or special dietary lessons in lacto-fermentation or gluten-free baking. Select from basic kitchen skills and beginners lessons and work your way up to more advanced cuisine creations.

Classes for kids aged nine and up will give you an extra pair of helping hands in the kitchen. Charlottesville Wine and Culinary offers a variety of options for the learning foodie. You can take a class as an individual on-site at Mona Lisa Pasta, or opt for instruction in your home—with or without friends. Have too many friends? Arrange a private class at a winery!

The Charlottesville Cooking School
2041 Barracks Rd., Charlottesville 22903
434-963-2665
www.charlottesvillecookingschool.com

Mona Lisa Pasta
921 Preston Ave., Charlottesville 22903
434-295-2494
www.monalisapasta.com

Charlottesville Wine and Culinary
434-974-7444
www.wineandculinary.com

Misty Mountain Camp Resort
56 Misty Mountain Rd., Greenwood 22943
540-456-6409
www.mistymountaincampresort.com

Shenandoah National Park
3655 E Highway 211, Luray 22835
540-999-3500
www.goshenandoah.com

TASTE BAGELS,
BETTER THAN NEW YORK'S

Outsiders call it blasphemy. C'villians call it the truth. Bodo's Bagels are the best, anywhere. Don't believe us? Then you haven't been there. Local tradition has it has a high honor to be the day's first customer with the coveted "#001" printed receipt. Can you get up that early?

Bodo's Bagels Locations:

1418 Emmet St.
434-977-9598

505 Preston Ave. (Downtown)
434-293-5224

1609 University Avenue (on the Corner)
434-293-6021

www.bodosbagels.com

TOUR THE VINEYARDS
OF CENTRAL VIRGINIA

Thomas Jefferson liked wine, and so does Charlottesville. Following the Monticello Wine Trail is a highly recommended activity any time of year, as a date, or with a group; it's not Napa, but it sure is fantastic. At last count there were more than 30 local wine makers, vineyards, and tasting rooms. Pace yourself; you don't need to visit all 30 in a single afternoon, but we recommend making a plan to get to each over time. Some are large, fancy venues, often the stage for elaborate weddings. Pippin Hill, King Family, Veritas, and Early Mountain fit this description and are great for larger group visits. More intimate venues, excellent for romantic dates and proposal spots, include Wisdom Oak, Cardinal Point, and Flying Fox.

Blue Ridge Wine Excursions provides the smart, comfortable way to experience the wine trail with no worries, suitable for accommodating a small to large group.

Each vineyard is as unique as the varietals they offer. Taste, buy, linger, and come back again and again to your favorite spots.

Monticello Wine Trail
www.monticellowinetrail.com

Blue Ridge Wine Excursions
853 W. Main St. #103, Charlottesville 22903
434-242-9313
blueridgewineexcursions.com

CRUISE FOR BREWS
ALONG THE BREWERY TRAIL

The Know Good Beer festival invites you to try two- or four-ounce samplings of regional and national beers, ciders, bourbons, and spirits at this extremely popular event. Annually, in the spring, at Ix Art Park, you can learn about brewing techniques, visit with other hops enthusiasts, eat local foods, and taste a wide variety of beers.

If the annual event isn't enough to wet your whistle (and really, how could it be?), there are several local breweries to visit. Our favorites? Champion Brewing Company, Devil's Backbone Brewing Company, Random Row Brewing Company, Blue Mountain Brewery, Starr Hill, and Three Notch'd Craft Kitchen and Brewery. Sign up for a public or private tour with C'ville Hop on Tours and your transportation is secure.

www.knowgoodbeer.com
cvillehopontours.com

Champion Brewing Company

324 6th St. SE, Charlottesville 22902
434-295-2739
championbrewingcompany.com

Devils Backbone Brewing Company

200 Mosbys Run, Roseland 22967
434-361-1001
www.dbbrewingcompany.com

Blue Mountain Brewery

9519 Critzer Shop Rd., Afton 22920
540-456-8020
www.bluemountainbrewery.com

Random Row Brewing Company

608 Preston Ave. A, Charlottesville 22902
434-284-8466
www.randomrow.com

Starr Hill

5391 Three Notch'd Rd., Crozet 22932
434-823-5671
www.starrhill.com

Three Notch'd Craft Kitchen and Brewery

520 Second Street SE, Charlottesville 22903
434-956-3141
threenotchdbrewing.com

TAKE TIME FOR TEA
AT THE SILVER THATCH INN

Historic bed and breakfast, the Silver Thatch Inn hosts vintage afternoon tea events most Saturdays and Sundays. Guests can indulge in endless pots of tea, warm scones with clotted cream, and finger sandwiches. Some tea-time events feature presentations from local history experts. It's an elegant way to spend a weekend afternoon with friends.

Silver Thatch Inn
3001 Hollymead Dr., 434-978-4686
http://silverthatch.com/afternoon-tea.htm

TRY BENELUX DINING
AT BRASSERIE SAISON

Have you ever heard the term "Benelux"? Nope, neither had we. It refers to a blend of Belgian and Dutch-inspired food culture that is wholly embraced by Charlottesville's only Downtown Mall restaurant and brewery. A collaboration between Ten Course Hospitality, the group that manages other favorite local restaurants such as The Whiskey Jar, The Pie Chest, and The Alley Light and Champion Brewing Company, Brasserie Saison offers a refined menu with small-batch beer pairings that will make you think you've skipped a couple of time zones for an authentic and special dining experience.

111 E. Main St., 434-202-7027
brasseriesaison.net

TIP
For an extra-special dining experience, book the tiny downstairs Coat Room with seating for up to eight guests. You'll enjoy wines and libations only available in the secret cozy lair and personal attention from the staff.

TRY A SLICE
IN A COLLEGE TOWN

What's a college town without awesome pizza? I don't ever want to find out. The Charlottesville area has five particularly popularly lauded pizza joints: Lampo Neopolitan Pizzeria, Mellow Mushroom, Crozet Pizza, Dr. Ho's Humble Pie, and Christian's Pizza. Each is unique in crust preparation, sauce flavor and allotment, topping selections, and overall ambiance. The only thing to do is try each one and choose your favorite.

Lampo Neopolitan Pizzeria

205 Monticello Road, Charlottesville 22902
434-244-3226

Mellow Mushroom

1321 W. Main St., Charlottesville 22903
434-972-9366

Crozet Pizza

5794 Three Notch'd Rd., Crozet 22932
434-823-2132
www.crozetpizza.com

Dr. Ho's Humble Pie

3586 Monacan Trail Rd., North Garden 22959
434-245-0000
www.doctorhoshumblepie.com

Christian's Pizza

Downtown: 118 W. Main St., Charlottesville 22902
434-977-9688

SIP YOUR TEA
AT TWISTED BRANCH TEA BAZAAR

If the coffee shop scene is not for you, the Twisted Branch Tea Bazaar might be. Tea connoisseurs and tobacco fans flock upstairs to the Downtown Mall's only tea bazaar and hookah bar for a caffeine rush and tobacco hit. It might seem odd, or dated, but the atmosphere is 1960s chic, and the crowd is there to study, work, visit with one another, or just ponder life. Seating is lush with cushions and pillows, small-group rooms, or a cozy outdoor patio. Don't harsh the mellow. Teas and hookahs of many flavors abound. This spot also plays host to musicians on occasion and offers vegetarian and vegan food items.

414 E. Main St., 434-293-9947
www.teabazaar.com

TIP
Check the schedule for live music events in the evenings and come back to the Tea Bazaar for a different kind of experience.

DINE AL FRESCO
ON THE DOWNTOWN MALL

Charlottesville's Downtown Mall is lined with fantastic restaurants, and many of them offer seasonal outdoor seating. If you do just one thing while in Charlottesville on a beautiful day, take the opportunity to eat lunch or dinner at a table on the bricks of the Mall. The people-watching is spectacular! The atmosphere is charming. You may be serenaded by a busker (talent not guaranteed). Locals flock to the outdoor tables on barely temperate days and stay there 'til the weather turns chilly again, sometime after Thanksgiving. We get what we can out of the opportunity to dine outdoors! Beware of overly tame squirrels that *will* approach you.

TIP
Nearly all the tables are spoken for—the property of restaurants who rent and maintain them. So it is decidedly not okay to plop down at any table with your brown bag lunch. If you do, you may get the boot.

MEET FOR COFFEE
AT A LOCAL SHOP

Charlottesvillians are fairly serious about their caffeine delivery mechanisms. Are the beans roasted in-house? Where did the coffee come from? Is it fair trade? What notes and aromas will I detect in the brewing? Is it French press, single-cup pour over, or vacuum brewed? Our local coffeehouses are some of our shining stars; try Mudhouse Downtown, Shenandoah Joe, and Milli Coffee Roasters for starters. Take a tour and taste-test your favorites. All are great places to work, drink multiple cups, and meet friends or colleagues—coffee is often an excuse for our community members to gather.

Mudhouse Downtown

213 W. Main St., Charlottesville 22902
434-984-6833
mudhouse.com

Shenandoah Joe

945 Preston Ave., Charlottesville 22903
434-295-4563
shenandoahjoe.com

Milli Coffee Roasters

400 Preston Ave. #150, Charlottesville 22903
434-282-2659
millicoffeeroasters.com

TAKE A SWEET TRIP
THROUGH THE CITY

It's possible, and recommended, to take a meandering walk from west to east of Downtown and hit four different bakeries along the way.

Start at MarieBette, a French bakery with petit kouign amann and financiers good enough to make you weep. Jog to the south to get to Albemarle Baking Company, where the Princess Cake is a birthday favorite for kids big and small. From there, travel east to Sweethaus Cupcake Café, where you can enjoy a stroll around Ix Art Park while you munch on a Black-Eyed Susan or, better yet, the Everything Cupcake! Take a hike up the hill and down West Second Street, burning calories as you go, and pop into Paradox Pastry Café to try a full-butter croissant or a slice of four-layer Guinness Chocolate cake. Continue over the train tracks and cross the Downtown Mall to reach The Pie Chest for a slice of Bourbon Pecan or Lemon Chess pie. By then you're going to need a nap, but we're sure you'll enjoy the voyage.

Sweethaus Cupcake Café

843 W. Main St., Charlottesville 22903
434-422-2677
www.sweethaus.com

MarieBette

700 Rose Hill Drive, Charlottesville 22903
434-529-6118
www.mariebette.com

Paradox Pastry Café

313 2nd St. SE #103, Charlottesville 22902
434-245-2253
www.paradoxpastrycafe.com

Albemarle Baking Company

418 West Main St., Charlottesville 22902
434-293-6456
www.albemarlebakingco.com

The Pie Chest

119 Fourth St. NE, Charlottesville 22902
434-977-0443
www.thepiechestcville.com

GREASE YOUR SPOON
AT THE WHITE SPOT

I wouldn't recommend making a visit to the White Spot a daily occurrence. Any diet would suffer from overindulgence in this historic burger joint's specialties, but once in a while, or even once in a lifetime, the Gus Burger is a must. A departure from the hifalutin' gourmet offerings of restaurants downtown or in Belmont, the White Spot steps back in time, to an era free from cholesterol concerns. Many a Gus Burger has been consumed as a late-night/early-morning meal, following what is often a Corner pub crawl. For many, the greasy spoon treatment is the perfect way to cure what ails ya. The Gus Burger, as fans know, is an all-beef patty topped with cheese and a fried egg. Add enhancements and fries as you see fit.

Inexpensive and worth the walk (there's rarely a place to park, but you'll need a walk before and after anyway), so plan to visit the Grounds, thoroughly explore the Corner, and treat yourself to some good, greasy eats.

1407 University Ave., 434-295-9899

TIP
If you're willing to take it up a notch, try the Motor Burger, which is a double cheeseburger, fried egg, and a thick slab of country ham.

STAKE YOUR CLAIM
ON THE CORNER

Just off the Grounds, the Corner is rich in history, shopping, restaurants, and student-influenced culture. Eat dinner at the Virginian! Have a Gus Burger at the White Spot! Grab a beer at Boylan Heights! Enjoy a cocktail at the rooftop bar of the Graduate Hotel! If you're ambitiously pursuing the completion of this list, get in touch with local historian and media personality Coy Barefoot, author of the book *The Corner: A History of Student Life at the University of Virginia*. Buy the book and use it as your roadmap to Corner shenanigans, or find Coy himself and rope him into giving you the personal tour.

MUSIC AND ENTERTAINMENT

FIND YOUR VENUE
FOR LIVE MUSIC

See a concert at one of several venues: the Jefferson Theatre, the Paramount, John Paul Jones Arena, or the nTelos Wireless Pavilion. Each spot has its own unique vibe. The Jefferson is a smaller, more intimate space, the Paramount a fancier, more formal, historic theatre. John Paul Jones Arena is where the University of Virginia holds its home basketball games, so expect big names like Dave Matthews (who got his start in a sketchy bar called Miller's on the Downtown Mall). The Pavilion, the white mushroom-shaped structure on the far east end of the Downtown Mall, is an outdoor venue for late spring through early fall entertainment. Each Friday in the summer, bands perform in the free series, Fridays After Five.

ENJOY LOCAL THEATRE
AT LIVE ARTS

Live Arts is just the ticket to scratch your theatrical itch. Participate in, or just be the audience for, Charlottesville's all-volunteer community theatre, established as long ago as 1990. The great thing about community theatre is just that; it's a true community collaboration. Live Arts brings together all-volunteer casts, producers, set builders, choreographers, and directors for some surprisingly well-done productions. Looking for a bargain? Try a "Pay What You Can" Wednesday evening performance, keeping in mind your donation helps keep the theatre alive.

In addition to year-round theatre productions, Live Arts offers programs and workshops to teach the arts to both adults and children.

123 E. Water St., 434-977-4177
www.livearts.org

WITNESS A SPECTACLE
AT CLAW

CLAW, otherwise known as Charlottesville Lady Arm Wrestlers, is wildly celebrated in our little town. We love our lady arm wrestlers! The names are as entertaining as the event (and the costumes). See the Homewrecker, Malice in Wonderland, Stiletto Southpaw, and Tropical Depression at their best! CLAW is a bunch of beefed up local gals with amazing guns competing for bragging rights and upper body strength mojo, all while raising money for charitable organizations in town. Part carnival sideshow, part theatrical spectacle, and, I suppose, part sporting event, our town's baddest ladies dress up and throw down for charity.

www.clawville.org

EMBARK ON A STAYCATION
IN CHARLOTTESVILLE

Stay at a boutique inn or bed and breakfast. Better yet, stay at home—someone else's. Stay Charlottesville allows you to "live like a local," making it possible to rent space in some pretty spectacular homes. Renovating? Escaping the in-laws? Or, if you are from somewhere else, there's nothing better than a short- or long-term stay in a finely appointed, perfectly situated property that is truly home (someone else's home, but for a time, and a price, yours). There are dozens of charming spots, both in town and in the country. Stay in one for a visit, or if you live in Charlottesville, find an excuse to spend a night away from home.

434-977-0442
www.staycharlottesville.com

CRASH A CONCERT
BY EAVESDROPPING FROM THE BELMONT BRIDGE

Concert tickets are costly. Prudent concert-goers need to pick and choose which acts to see. If you're on the fence, here's an alternative. Stand on the sidewalk just to the north of the Belmont Bridge on Avon Street, behind the nTelos Wireless Pavilion on the far east end of the Downtown Mall, and enjoy a concert. Commune with the other freeloaders in a unique experience of enjoying the backstage pass of a concert for free.

Big acts pack the sidewalk, so determine your crowd comfort level before you go, and plan to move along if authorities request it.

HANG OUT
AT MILLER'S

If you think you're a Dave Matthews Band fan, then you probably know that legendary local singer got his start working at and playing Miller's, a somewhat seedy bar on the Downtown Mall. Miller's has great bar food, but the ambiance is strictly saloon. The 30-plus-old hangout boasts a third-floor pool room and a full kitchen open 'til midnight. Go for live music, beer, and well drinks. And as a DMB fan, revel in the historic significance of Charlottesville's favorite musical son.

109 W. Main St., 434-971-8511
www.millersdowntown.com

TRY BOARD GAMES
WITH A LOCAL CONNECTION

You may have heard of the board game Settlers of Catan, but you probably weren't aware that the business of the game is managed in Charottesville by Catan Studio. With more than 27 million sold, and worldwide competitions held in Germany each year, it comes as a surprise to enthusiasts that the brand is run right here in central Virginia. Players of the game take the role of settlers: acquiring resources, trading, and building civilizations to earn points and win.

A new, less well known board game from another company with local roots is Chickapig. With Kickstarter funding and support from its owner's friend Dave Matthews, Chickapig is sweeping the nation. It's fun, silly, strategic, and involves chicken-pig hybrids, cows, and lots of cow poop. Kardinal Hall, a downtown beer garden and restaurant, has Chickapig Tuesdays, where anyone can come to learn and play.

www.catan.com
chickapig.com
kardinalhall.com

GO BACK TO HIGH SCHOOL
JUST FOR A NIGHT

It's OK—it's only temporary. The award-winning orchestra at Charlottesville High School is worth a listen. Nationally recognized for excellence, the orchestra has 150 members and comprises a string ensemble and a concert orchestra. Supported, in part, through the generosity of the Boyd Tinsley Fund (if you're from Charlottesville you know that Boyd Tinsley is the noteworthy violinist famous for his role in the Dave Matthews Band). The orchestra has taken top prizes at music festivals in London, New York, Boston, Atlanta, and Chicago, to name just a few.

Not to be overshadowed by the city's high school, Albemarle High School has an equally recognized drama department. The spring musical at AHS is a widely attended production with much more than parents and fellow students filling the auditorium for every sold-out performance—it's a real community-wide event. Two consecutive years have had the community at-large voting the AHS musical as the favorite local play—of all the theatres, of all the plays in town—in a weekly publication's annual poll.

Charlottesville High School

1400 Melbourne Rd., Charlottesville 22901
434-245-2410
chsorchestra.org

Albemarle High School

2775 Hydraulic Rd., Charlottesville 22901
434-975-9300
ahsplayers.webs.com

Western Albemarle High School

5941 Rockfish Gap Turnpike, Crozet 22932
434-823-8700
www2.k12albemarle.org/school/WAHS

Monticello High School

1400 Independence Way, Charlottesville 22902
434-244-3100
www.k12albemarle.org/monticello

SUPPORT THE DERBY DAMES

There is nothing like a dame, declares the song in the musical *South Pacific*, and we agree. Charlottesville's Derby Dames are amazing bruisers on skates, bringing feminine wiles to the roller derby track in fishnets, lipstick, helmets, and elbow pads. The ladies of the rink engage in good sportsmanship while slamming around the flat track playing with roller derby rules. The sisterhood formed by the Derby Dames is one of support, athleticism, adrenaline, and strength. If you're intrigued, sign up to be Fresh Meat, the euphemism for newbies just getting their derby legs. Supporting the Dames is easy—come witness a bout; volunteer as a referee, coach, or trainer; or just eat at Blue Moon Diner on designated days when 10 percent of the take goes to the Dames.

www.charlottesvillederbydames.com

DRINK WITH GEEKS
AT TRIVIA NIGHT

Geeks Who Drink have chapters all over the country. In the Charlottesville group, you can join a live trivia night every Tuesday night at Blue Mountain Brewery. Put your brains to the test over some local brew and go head to head with other smarty-pants locals. Prizes can be won!

www.geekswhodrink.com/40/Charlottesville

Blue Mountain Brewery
9519 Critzer Shop Rd., Afton 22920
540-456-8020
www.bluemountainbrewery.com

GO TO THE RACES
AT FOXFIELD

Foxfield Races has two events, one in the spring and the other in the fall. They are two very different experiences while still being horse races at Foxfield.

Families will enjoy the fall event—kids eight and under are free and can jump in a bounce house, go on pony rides, and visit the kids' tent when racing horses fail to impress. It's a low-key family event.

The spring Foxfield races have another reputation entirely. Commemorated by the annual television news story featuring drunk and sometimes underage attendees being loaded into paddy wagons, Foxfield in the spring is a bacchanalia of 25,000 participants in cute sundresses and Wellington boots drinking far too many cocktails. Oh yeah, and there are horses racing.

At Free Union and Garth Rds., 434-293-9501
www.foxfieldraces.com

VIEW GREAT FLICKS
AT THE VIRGINIA FILM FESTIVAL

Each year in early November Charlottesville plays host to Hollywood. A long weekend is packed with more than 100 films, including independent films, fascinating documentaries, feature debuts, classics, Virginia filmmakers, and exciting special guests. Famous producers, actors, and directors make appearances at the Virginia Film Festival, speaking at screenings of their films, and making themselves available for audience interaction. The annual lineup announcement is eagerly anticipated, and guests buy their tickets well in advance to ensure good seats.

www.virginiafilmfestival.org

CATCH A SHOW
AT A HISTORIC THEATRE

The historic Paramount Theater should be on your list of places to visit downtown. It's a beautifully restored theatre in the middle of the Charlottesville Downtown Mall. The venue is used for concerts, ballets, operas, speakers, nonprofit galas, and more. An event at the Paramount always feels very special. Visit the Paramount around the holidays for a special movie night featuring a classic like *It's a Wonderful Life* or *White Christmas*. Take the afternoon for holiday shopping before this annual family movie tradition. When you emerge from the theatre into the dark amid the marquee lights and the crisp cold of December (and, if you're lucky, a few picturesque snowflakes falling), there's no chance you'll be able to escape the holiday spirit.

The Paramount
215 E. Main St., 434-979-1922
www.theparamount.net

TAKE OFF EARLY
FOR A FREE CONCERT

From mid-April to mid-September, enjoy a free concert in a very family friendly atmosphere. Fridays After Five is this town's favorite live concert series. The audience is populated with people just getting off work, as well as whole families enjoying a night out in the summertime weather. Concessions are available for al fresco dinner options. The lawn at the Pavilion is a favorite hangout for dancing toddlers and their moms. It's a great way to greet neighbors and friends, hear some (often local) music, and start off the weekend with a community celebration.

Summer Fridays

nTelos Wireless Pavilion
700 E. Main St., 434-245-4910
www.thenteloswirelesspavilion.com

GET OUT
OF AN IMMERSION ESCAPE ROOM

An entertainment trend sweeping the nation is the puzzle-solving adventure of an immersive experience. Gather your team and prepare to solve puzzles, crack codes, and find hidden objects in an escape room adventure. There are three different custom-built rooms to try, giving you the chance to make multiple visits with family, co-workers or friends. For the claustrophobic, the room isn't truly locked (that would be unsafe) but the illusion is real! Give over your disbelief and focus on using teamwork, strategy, and creativity to gain your escape.

The experience can be a little intense for kids under age 16. Children under the age of 18 must be accompanied by a parent.

Immersion Escape Rooms
2125 Ivy Rd., 434-249-8797
www.immersionescaperooms.com

LET'S ALL GO
TO THE MOVIES

Until 2012, Charlottesville seemed like the last small town in America without a state-of-the-art multiplex with an IMAX theater and stadium seating. In short order, the area gained three with separate personalities: Stonefield, Violet Crown, and Alamo Drafthouse. Stonefield is a huge, mainstream, blockbuster-hosting movie theater. Violet Crown, our Downtown Mall theatre, offers reserved seating, small-theatre experiences with beer, wine, and food available to take in with you. Alamo Drafthouse also has reserved seating, and waiters will serve you food and drinks right at your seat! Residents have rejoiced, after suffering from long-outdated theaters. Now we feel even better than the rest of America, plunking down $100–$200 for a family of four to see the latest action adventure film.

Regal Stonefield Stadium and IMAX
1954 Swanson Dr., 434-244-3213
www.shopsatstonefield.com

Violet Crown Charlottesville
200 W. Main Street, 434-529-3000
charlottesville.violetcrown.com

Alamo Drafthouse
375 Merchant Walk Square, 434-326-5056
drafthouse.com/Charlottesville

EXPERIENCE AUTHENTIC SHAKESPEARE

Just down the road, over the mountain, and into the valley, Staunton, Virginia, is home to the American Shakespeare Center and the Blackfriars' Playhouse. Known as the American home of Shakespeare, this excellent theatre is the world's only full recreation of Shakespeare's indoor theatre. The actors perform in historically accurate theatre space with no elaborate sets, no microphones or speakers, and with the actors sharing the same lighting as the audience. It's a unique experience of Elizabethan work and just a short drive from Downtown Charlottesville.

The Blackfriars' Playhouse
10 S. Market St., Staunton 24401
540-851-1733
www.americanshakespearecenter.com

TIP

Make time to walk around downtown Staunton, where you'll find charming shops, excellent restaurants, and beautiful homes.

GAZE AT THE STARS
AT VERITAS WINERY

Just ask Van Gogh: wine and starry nights are a perfect pairing. Veritas Winery takes it a step further and adds live music to the mix. A popular summertime event, Starry Nights at Veritas invites guests to bring lawn chairs and blankets and sit out under the great big expanse of sky while enjoying live music and wonderful Veritas wines.

151 Veritas Lane, Afton 22920
540-456-8000
www.veritaswines.com/events.php

STRETCH YOUR
MUSIC MUSCLES

This town is full of talent and people who like to pass it on. Music lessons at the Front Porch run the gamut from guitar to banjo, African drumming to fiddle. Around the corner from the Front Porch, you can take voice lessons in a studio right on the Downtown Mall at the Center for Vocal Study. When you're satisfied you have a single, head to the Music Resource Center to record your tracks and hit the big time.

More seasoned musicians will find fellowship in open jams at the Front Porch and performance opportunities at places like C'ville Coffee and the Batesville Market. When it comes to music, there are many opportunities to learn and share.

The Front Porch
221 Water St., 434-806-7062
frontporchcville.org

The Center for Vocal Study
114 E. Main St. Suite 300, 434-326-0797
Centerforvocalstudy.com

SEE A TINY CONCERT
IN THE GARAGE

In what must be the tiniest concert venue, a brick one-car garage faces a hill in a park in Downtown Charlottesville. During the day, it doesn't look like much, but on a concert night, the Garage transforms. Fans plop down on the grass in Lee Park and face the open garage where bands set up shop and entertain everyone within earshot. The Garage is on First Street between Market and Jefferson streets, next to the Hill and Wood Funeral Parlor. Aside from concerts, the Garage sometimes hosts art openings or potluck dinners. A Kickstarter success story, the venue was able to raise more than $10,000 to repair a hole in a brick wall and make needed improvements to the interior in 2013. Clearly, this is a spot well-loved by the C'ville community.

100 Jefferson St.
thegarage-cville.com

TIP

Bring ground cover and sit on the hill in the park opposite the Garage for stellar VIP seating.

APPLAUD SINGER/ SONGWRITER NIGHT
AT THE LOCAL

On Monday nights for years, Belmont restaurant the Local has played host to a collection of singer/songwriters for a talent show of, yes, locals backed by a house band. Each performer has the stage for just two songs, and regulars come back week after week. Come early, have a delicious dinner made with locally sourced foods, and when the entertainment begins at 9 p.m., you'll have a good seat. Fortunately for us, Charlottesville has attracted some truly talented singers and songwriters. Listen to a gathering of the best in town for a special evening of entertainment that doesn't cost a thing. But, naturally, the Local would prefer it if you would buy a drink or two and some food—and you should!

824 Hinton Ave., 434-984-9749
www.thelocal-cville.com

TIP

New singer/songwriters are always welcome and should sign up as soon as they arrive. It's not a competitive event; it's just a chance to share your art and talent, and get feedback on a piece in development. It's good for everyone, and really, what else have you got to do on a Monday night?

LEARN TO DANCE
WITH C'VILLE SAVOY

Dancers know that any kind of dance movement is a great workout under the cover of great fun. C'ville Savoy hosts dance education and gatherings the fourth Saturday of every month. Learn Lindy Hop (Swing) from teachers patient enough to coach beginners. Every gathering begins with lessons for an hour, followed by social dancing into the night. To my great delight, as a bonus, the dance community teaches interested folks how to do the Thriller dance (from Michael Jackson's famous song and video of the same name) near the end of every October.

313 2nd St. SE #108, 434-260-0059
www.swingcville.org/cvillesavoy.php

CRASH A WEDDING

Weddings are big business in Charlottesville and Albemarle County. In fact, Charlottesville is considered a popular destination for wedding parties. In incredible numbers, brides who don't live in Charlottesville choose to have their weddings with the breathtaking backdrop of the Blue Ridge Mountains. Try, if you can, to get invited to a Central Virginia wedding. If not, crash one, and see what all the fuss is about.

SPORTS AND RECREATION

GO UP IN THE AIR
IN A HOT AIR BALLOON

Conditions must be right for this high-altitude treat, and it's not recommended for anyone who isn't reasonably fit or who is afraid of heights. On a low-wind day, if those obstacles are settled, the vista of the Blue Ridge Mountains, the lush green of Southern horse farms, and sleepy rivers cannot be beat. A gently rising and coasting hot air balloon is the only way to enjoy the slow-moving, high-level perspective of the area.

434-589-6213
www.blueridgeballoon.com
www.virginiahotairballoon.com

WATCH POLO
AT KING FAMILY VINEYARDS

Before I lived in Virginia, I'd never seen a polo game—televised or live. Polo is a sport often showcased by a well-heeled kind of community that only East Coast towns seem to boast. It is, in part, an excuse for women to don a sundress and an otherwise-ridiculous-if-worn-anywhere-else hat. Wear shoes suitable for divot stomping—the halftime practice of tamping down the torn-up turf. It's a popular tradition, and people of all ages will take to the field to stomp around. Make sure you're paying attention when the athletes and the horses want to get back on the field, or the lawn may not be the only thing that gets stomped! Polo matches are free and open to the public. Wine is *not* free, but tastings and a shared bottle or two are recommended. Try the Viognier, made from the state grape of Virginia. There's nothing that will make you feel more like a part of the upper echelon than sipping a glass of Viognier while observing a polo match (with rules you barely understand), in the shadow of the Blue Ridge Mountains.

6550 Roseland Farm, Crozet 22932
434-823-7800
www.kingfamilyvineyards.com

FLOAT, KAYAK, OR CANOE
ON A RIVER

Easy access to the Rivanna, the James, and the Shenandoah rivers is nearby, and several rental companies can hook you up with the necessary equipment if you don't own your own. A day trip of four hours or so leaves plenty of time to play in the water and picnic on the beach. Make sure you have lifejackets—rivers are monitored by local police and not having a flotation device may earn you a hefty fine. It's also important to pay attention to river levels. A lot of rain may make the river levels too high and unsafe; a drought can make them too low and not much fun. A summer without spending time on one of Central Virginia's peaceful rivers simply isn't a summer at all.

virginiarivers.org

RIDE YOUR BIKE
THROUGH THE SCENIC COUNTRYSIDE

Bicyclists enjoy many excellent scenic routes in and around Charlottesville. The route from Edge Valley Road to Plank Road is a favorite. This ride is more than 2.7 miles of valley, first settled in the eighteenth century. Edge Valley Road runs from Taylor's Gap Road at its eastern end to historic Plank Road to the west. The ride begins with views of a stunning, century-old Georgian manor home and the remains of an ancient cabin. Follow along the Middlebranch North Fork Hardware River in picture-perfect countryside, passing marshy wetlands and an artist's vision of an old red barn in the middle of a rolling hay field. Roll into Batesville, an unincorporated community in Albemarle County founded in 1760. In pre–Civil War days, the town was a station on the direct path for agricultural goods to get to eastern customers. At Batesville, you can go left to Pippin Hill Winery for a visit to the tasting room, then on to Dr. Ho's Humble Pie to finish the day off right.

www.bikecharlottesville.org

TAKE YOUR DOG
FOR A ROMP

Charlottesville is definitely a town for dog lovers, with a well-supported no-kill animal shelter and many pet-friendly venues. But nothing delights a dog more than a romp in a dog park with fellow furry friends. Dog parks are at Darden Towe Park, Riverview Park, Azalea Park, and Chris Greene Lake.

On a relatively dry weekend afternoon, pack up the dog, or borrow one (or two—but not three—there are rules about these things) if you don't have your own, and head out to the Chris Greene Lake dog park. It's hard to be grumpy in the presence of bounding, fetching, and joyous animals. The first time I stumbled upon the dog park on a hike I was sans canine but still visited to watch all the pups playing. Dog people are, generally, friendly, and there's a ready-made topic of conversation as your animals sniff each other.

Darden Towe Park

1445 Darden Towe Park, Charlottesville 22911
434-296-5911

Riverview Park

End of Chesapeake Street at the eastern city limits

Azalea Park

Off Old Lynchburg Road at the southern edge of the
city near Interstate 64.

Chris Greene Lake

4748 Chris Greene Lake Rd., Charlottesville 22911
434-296-5844

WALK THE GROUNDS,
STREAK THE LAWN

College campuses are often beautiful, and the Grounds at the University of Virginia are no exception. The Grounds of UVA (don't call it campus!) feature beautiful historic buildings, manicured lawns, picturesque trees, elegant gardens, and a fantastic serpentine wall. Make sure you take a guided tour with at least an alumnus if not a currently enrolled student. Don't miss Edgar Allan Poe's room, the Lawn, its pavilions and their surrounding rooms of upper-echelon students, the Amphitheatre, and the Rotunda.

Of course, we can't recommend that anyone disrobe and run across the Lawn, the pristine yard in front of the Rotunda, but some say the tradition at the University of Virginia includes just that—streaking during the first snowfall of winter, specifically. Use your own good judgment, or recognize that the tradition exists and strategically time a walk on the Grounds to see if you can spot a traditionalist.

www.virginia.edu

TAKE A WALK IN THE WOODS
ALONG THE APPALACHIAN TRAIL

The book *A Walk in the Woods: Rediscovering America on the Appalachian Trail*, by Bill Bryson, could inspire just about anyone to lace up those hiking boots and hit the trail. The book documents a pair's journey on the A.T., a trail that stretches from Georgia to Maine. Plenty of miles of the A.T. run through Virginia, and particularly through the Charlottesville area. If you don't have time to hike the entire A.T., get a local taste and perhaps you'll be inspired to try the full trip one day. For the less ambitious, there are other, shorter hikes with big payoffs of vistas, waterfalls, or just plain beautiful scenery. The important thing is to get out on a trail, for a little bit or a long time, somewhere in the area. You won't be sorry.

Hikes we like include Humpback Rocks, Old Rag, Spy Rock, Crabtree Falls, Sugar Hollow, Blue Hole, and the Rivanna Trail. Riverview Park, close to downtown, is good if you're short on time and can't get to the country.

SIT ON A TRACTOR SEAT
AT THE TOP OF BEAR DEN MOUNTAIN

Walk the trail at Bear Den Mountain in Shenandoah National Park and end up at the top of the mountain where a semicircle of tractor seats have been planted in the ground. The family that owned the land put them there (no, we can't grow tractor seats in Virginia soil), and there they've stayed for decades. Have a seat and admire the view of the Blue Ridge Mountains.

Bear Den Trail Center
18393 Blueridge Mountain Rd., Bluemont 20135
540-554-8708
www.bearsdencenter.org

FLY AWAY
FROM THE CHARLOTTESVILLE-ALBEMARLE AIRPORT

Depart from the most wonderful regional airport you'll ever experience. It's a five-gate, two-story building with one security line (often with no one in it) and a clean, small, comfortable boarding area. It's as no-hassle a commercial flying experience as you can get with a beautiful view out the wall of windows overlooking the runway to admire while you wait. While you're at the airport, ride the only escalator in Charlottesville or Albemarle County. Take a single jump to get to Chicago, Atlanta, Charlotte, Washington, D.C., New York, or Philadelphia. From there, the sky's the limit!

100 Bowen Loop, 434-973-8342
www.gocho.com

BE A YOGI

Hatha, Ashtanga, Bikram Yoga, Hot Yoga, or Pilates: Charlottesville is a yoga town. In fact, about 40 miles south of town you'll find Yogaville, home to the Satchidananda Ashram and a community of people devoted to the teachings of Integral Yoga. In town, there are numerous opportunities to get your yoga fix—hot yoga, beginners' yoga, reformer Pilates, and more. First, shop for your yoga outfits at Lululemon or the Hip Joint, then get down to being bendy at the yoga hangout of your choice.

Lululemon

109 2nd St. SE, Charlottesville 22903
434-982-8826
shop.lululemon.com

The Hip Joint

110 2nd St. NE #201, Charlottesville 22902
434-971-6888
www.thehipjointdances.com

Yogaville

108 Yogaville Way, Buckingham 23921
800-858-9642
www.yogaville.org

ALL ABOARD
AMTRAK

Take a train. Sometimes the best thing to do in Charlottesville is get out of Charlottesville. Amtrak makes it super easy. You can pop up to D.C. without breaking a sweat. Board the train on a Friday afternoon and get to NYC as the clubs are starting to hop. Great weekends await in Washington, D.C., Philadelphia, Boston, and New York—in an inexpensive, low-stress way to travel. With the station located downtown, university students and visitors can come and go easily and working commuters can zip around the northeast working with onboard Wi-Fi in total comfort.

810 West Main St., 434-296-4559
www.amtrak.com

GET FIT
AT FABULOUS FACILITIES

Get your butt kicked, or kick your own butt, at Crossfit or MADabolic. Charlottesville is lousy with overachievers. I blame the University of Virginia and Thomas Jefferson, personally, who allegedly said, "You should spend at least two hours a day on bodily exercise." If you subscribe to that philosophy, it's easy to achieve this goal with a plethora of gyms, health clubs, classes, groups, and instructors to get you on your healthy way. Crossfit and Madabolic are two boutique options for getting your fitness fix.

Crossfit calls itself a fitness community. Fans enjoy the culture of small-group training from a certified instructor and the inspiration that comes from a competitive atmosphere. MADabolic is an innovative, interval-driven strength and endurance program with 50-minute-long classes offered each day. There's a fitness option for everyone in Charlottesville. Find yours and get in your two hours (or 50 minutes) a day!

Crossfit
1309 Belleview Ave. #2, 434-260-0209
www.crossfitcharlottesville.com

MADabolic
943 2nd Street NE, 434-989-3345
www.madabolic.com

ROW YOUR BOAT
ON THE RIVANNA RESERVOIR

Anyone who has tried a rowing machine at the gym knows that rowing is a great workout. Actually rowing in the water is even better. You can learn to row the right way in beautiful surroundings on the Rivanna reservoir. The Rivanna Rowing Club offers a variety of programs, from the beginner-targeted Learn-to-Row classes to personal coaching for the seasoned sculling team. Early risers will like getting out on the water before work—others will prefer the late-afternoon classes. Everyone, however, will get into shape. Programs are available for junior rowers (13 to 18 years of age) and adults. Boats and equipment provided.

www.rivannarowing.org

CAMP OR GLAMP
IN THE GREAT OUTDOORS

Camping is, admittedly, not for everyone. If it's your bag, however, Central Virginia is a great place to do it. Our weather is mild enough that there's easily three full seasons of comfortable camping with the right gear. RV camping, cabin camping, and full-on glamping (a.k.a. glamorous camping with every amenity a camper can have) are also available at several campgrounds in the region. Two favorites: Misty Mountain Resort is great for families and allows for a downright affordable staycation. The resort is great for RVs or tents and offers a pool, a spray park, ziplines, canoe and kayak rental, wine and brewery tours, and all the outdoor amenities your camping heart desires.

Camping spots are plentiful in Shenandoah National Park, naturally, and backcountry camping is available by permit for the truly adventurous. If you're the tamer type, look into the four campgrounds with various options: Mathews Arm, Big Meadows, Lewis Mountain, and Loft Mountain. All have access to well-maintained hiking trails with visits to spectacular waterfalls. For the comfort camper, look into a stay at the Lodge at Big Meadows or a cabin at Skyland Resort and enjoy the historic surroundings in style.

CHEER FOR THE 'HOOS
NO MATTER YOUR SPORT

The University of Virginia offers more than just world-class education. You may have heard of their sports teams as well, famous for football, basketball, baseball, field hockey, golf, tennis, squash, and much, much more! Pick your sport, buy your tickets, and be a fan. In Charlottesville, we call our fans and the athletes Wahoos, or 'Hoos—for short—at UVA. Officially, UVA's mascot and teams are the Cavaliers, but at games the customary yell is "Wahoowa!" Wear blue and orange and you'll fit right in!

www.virginiasports.com

SNUGGLE A BABY GOAT
AT CAROMONT FARM

Sometimes all a baby goat needs is a snuggle. Gail Hobbs-Page runs a goat dairy and cheese-making operation at Caromont Farm, where more than 30,000 pounds of cheese per year are produced. Good cheese happens when goats are happy. To socialize baby goats and prepare them for milking, Gail asks for visitors to take tours, learn about and buy her delicious cheese, and yes, snuggle a goat. Gail's original call for goat cuddlers went viral, causing an overwhelming influx of volunteers. Now the planned snuggle sessions sell out far in advance. We highly recommend the experience; adorable baby goat antics will put a smile on your face, and Gail's selection of award-winning cheeses will likely fill your tummy and your take-away bag.

9261 Old Green Mountain Rd., Esmont
434-831-1393
caromontcheese.com

HIT THE LINKS
AT A LOCAL GOLF COURSE

Keswick, Meadowcreek, Birdwood, Spring Creek, Farmington, Old Trail, and Glenmore—what are these hifalutin' sounding names? Why, golf courses, of course. Our greens are great, and golf enthusiasts love to get out and play 18 holes whenever weather permits. A few are private (Glenmore, Keswick, Farmington), so you'll have to find a member to let you play, but the rest are public, so step on up to the tee and swing away.

Keswick Club

701 Club Dr., Keswick 22947
434-923-4363, www.keswickclub.com

Meadowcreek Golf Club

1400 Pen Park Rd., Charlottesville 22901
434-977-0615, www.meadowcreekgolf.org

Birdwood Golf Course

410 Golf Course Dr., Charlottesville 22903
434-293-4653, www.boarsheadinn.com/Golf

Spring Creek Golf Club

109 Clubhouse Way, Gordonsville 22942
540-832-0744, www.springcreekgolfclub.com

Farmington Country Club

1625 Country Club Circle, Charlottesville 22901
434-296-5661, www.farmingtoncc.com

Old Trail Golf Club

5494 Golf Dr., Crozet 22932
434-823-8101, www.oldtrailgolf.com

Glenmore Country Club

1750 Piper Way, Charlottesville 22902
434-977-0701

CELEBRATE BATTEAU DAY
ALONG THE JAMES RIVER

The James River Festival celebrates a little-known local holiday known as Batteau Day. Batteaux are flat-bottomed wooden boats once used to transport tobacco, grains, and other goods down the James River. The boats, traditionally about eight feet wide and about 50 feet long, are reconstructed by historic interpreters. Reenactors and enthusiasts in traditional dress navigate the bateaux downriver from Lynchburg to Richmond, stopping where the river bends in Scottsville for a celebration with live music, crafts, food, and fun.

www.scottsville.org/batteau-festival

CRUISE SKYLINE DRIVE
TO SEE STUNNING VIEWS

The finest views of the Shenandoah Valley are displayed with breathtaking vistas best viewed from along Skyline Drive. This 105-mile route winds from Front Royal, Virginia, to Rockfish Gap, Virginia, and is one of the most spectacular ways to enjoy the fall foliage or the spring bloom. A meticulously planned roadway, Skyline Drive has 75 overlooks. Pack a picnic and plan to relax and enjoy several stops along the journey.

www.visitskylinedrive.org/Home.aspx

VISIT SHENANDOAH NATIONAL PARK
FOR OUTDOOR ADVENTURE

There are so very many reasons to visit Shenandoah National Park. Hiking, camping, exploring, spelunking, and nature watching are just some of the ways to spend time in the park. Catch a glimpse of black bears, deer, reptiles, amphibians, birds, and more. People have lived in the region of the park for more than 9,000 years, but the camp was created between 1933 and 1942 as a project of Franklin Delano Roosevelt's Civilian Conservation Corps.

3655 E. Highway 211, Luray 22835
540-999-3500
www.nps.gov/shen/index.htm

CHALLENGE YOURSELF
AT TRIPLE C CAMP

If you're looking for a challenge, or a way to bring a team of people closer together, the challenge course is a great choice. Feel like a kid at camp (because, essentially, you will be) at Triple C Camp's challenge course. From ziplines to climbing towers, you'll test your limits in the great outdoors with certified trainers and well-maintained facilities.

920 Camp Rd., 434-293-2529
www.tripleccamp.com

GET BOWLED OVER
AT KEGLER'S LANES

Go bowling at AMF Kegler's Lanes for a date, with the family, or with a group. One of the great things about living in a small town is that there's no confusion when you say to friends, "Meet me at the bowling alley!" AMF is north on I-29 in Albemarle County, and lucky for bowling enthusiasts all over the region, they do it right. There's plenty of space, with 48 lanes, a billiards room, video games, and a lounge. It's great for parties or a rainy afternoon with the kids, and friendly to everyone from very serious league bowlers to the totally casual bowler (that's me).

2000 Seminole Trail, 434-978-3999
amf.com/keglerslanes

GO BEYOND THE RUNWAY
AT THE CHARLOTTESVILLE-ALBEMARLE AIRPORT

Charlottesville-Albemarle Regional Airport is passenger friendly to be sure, but the airport known as CHO is a pretty great community member as well. Contact the airport to get a behind-the-scenes tour of emergency services, baggage claim, private aircraft, the runway extension, and places normally reserved for pilots and staff. It's a crowd pleaser for young kids and school groups, who will enjoy learning about airport operations and seeing aircraft up close. Grownups dig it, too—in an age when air travel is sometimes prohibitive, and security measures are extremely tight, it's nice to see what airport operations look like from the inside, and to stand on the tarmac without worrying about flight delays.

100 Bowen Loop, 434-973-8342
www.gocho.com

GET TUBULAR
ON THE JAMES RIVER

Tubing on the James River is a summertime tradition, but it's not for the faint of heart. I've canoed and kayaked, whitewater rafted and sailed. Nothing, however, compares to the lazy living that is floating in a tube down the James River. It is one part cultural spectacle, one part nature appreciation, and one part shenanigans. The requirements for a successful tubing day include an early start and a stockpile of your favorite beer in a cooler with snacks, sandwiches, and whatever other provisions you'll need to sustain you for a five-mile float downriver.

Do yourself a favor and engage James River Runners. They'll take you upriver by bus and provide life vests, tubes, and guidance for a successful river floating experience.

James River Runners
10092 Hatton Ferry Rd., Scottsville 24590
434-286-2338
www.jamesriver.com

NOTE

The cultural spectacle includes fellow floaters in a variety of swim attire, with a range of capacity for adult beverages, most consumed on the water in the form of cans of beer or vodka-infused Jell-O shots. You'll see a variety of questionable behaviors on the float downriver, so think carefully about whether you make this trip a family event. Drunken shenanigans are a standard feature on the float, and if your tolerance for foul language, beer swilling, and bikini clad girls and tattoos is low, you might want to stay on dry land.

RUN FROM ZOMBIES
IN A CREEPY 5K

One of the most hilarious and creepy events to witness/participate in is the Danger! Zombies! Run! 5K. If you're prepared to enter this late-October tradition, you have a choice to make: zombie or human? Humans get a 90-second headstart, which is appropriate, being among the living and all. But then, here come the zombies; other runners in full zombie makeup and attire chase the human runners through Downtown Charlottesville. Zombies must steal human runners' "lifelines"—the race is won by the fastest human and the zombie with the most "kills." If you're a human who gets killed during the race, don't worry; you're now a zombie and can chase humans the rest of the route. It's a crazy, scary good time.

www.badtothebone.biz

GO FISH
WITH ALBEMARLE ANGLER

There's plenty of good fishing to be done in the mountain streams of Virginia. Make sure you catch some by engaging an expert. Local outfit Albemarle Angler has experienced fly fishing guides who know the area's waterways, best techniques, equipment, and the secret hangouts of aquatic friends. Whether on your own or with a guide, you'll need a fishing license (we don't just let anyone catch our swimming dinners).

1129 Emmet St. N., 434-977-6882
albemarleangler.com

Photo courtesy Brantley Ussery

CULTURE AND HISTORY

MEET THE THIRD PRESIDENT
OF THE UNITED STATES

No matter what your GPS voice says, I'll tell you the truth: It's pronounced "Mont-eh-chell-o." CH! Like cello, the instrument. Say "Mont-i-sell-o" and you might be escorted out of the state. Anyone who has ever been to Charlottesville will tell you to visit Thomas Jefferson's home. It's Charlottesville's main attraction: the home designed and built by the father of the University of Virginia, the principal author of the Declaration of Independence, and the third president of the United States. The best way to experience Monticello is with an Evening Signature tour. This exclusive-access pass will give you an expert's tour of the remarkable gardens and the off-limits third-floor Dome Room. Even the most casual gardener will be fascinated by the history, planning, and cultivation of the plantation's self-sustaining gardens.

931 Thomas Jefferson Parkway, 434-984-9800
www.monticello.org

TIPS

The Fourth of July is Monticello's
big day. The U.S. Citizens' Naturalization
Ceremony is a highlight and features an
impressive speaker, along with an incredibly
moving ceremony that will give any
American a dose of patriotic pride.

Locals who can prove with an I.D. that they
live in Charlottesville can get in for free
when bringing a guest.

EXERCISE YOUR RIGHT
TO FREEDOM OF SPEECH

Write something thoughtful or crazy on the Freedom of Speech Wall, a community chalkboard (chalk provided) and monument to the First Amendment. Declare your unrequited love. Scrawl song lyrics. Draw a funny or serious picture. Take time to read what others have written. Be inspired, moved, offended, or amused. Then come back again in a week or so and read, write, or draw something entirely different. (The monument is "refreshed" twice a week.)

Thomas Jefferson Center for the Protection of Free Expression
605 E. Main St., 434-295-4784
www.tjcenter.org/monument

READ SOME POE
AND SEE HIS DORM ROOM

Pick up a book of Edgar Allan Poe's—I recommend anything including "The Raven" or "Annabel Lee." Take it with you and visit the hermetically sealed room preserved on the Grounds of the University of Virginia where the poet lived and was the writer-in-residence for a time in 1826. Conduct a live reading, either with or without an audience. Give yourself the creeps, if possible. Bonus points if you bring kids with you and can adequately creep them out as well.

McCormick Rd., UVA Campus
West Range #13, Charlottesville 22902

RIDE THE TROLLEY
FROM THE GROUNDS TO DOWNTOWN

Charlottesville Area Transit (CAT) offers a free trolley from the Downtown Transit Station along West Main Street to Jefferson Park Avenue, over to Scott Stadium and through UVA Grounds and back downtown. The trolley runs every day of the week and is a handy transportation option for students and townies alike. It is the cheapest, easiest way to get between downtown and UVA, particularly if you lack wheels of your own.

615 Water St. E., 434-970-3649
www.charlottesville.org/catchthecat

EXPLORE AFRICAN-AMERICAN HISTORY
AT THE JEFFERSON SCHOOL AFRICAN-AMERICAN HERITAGE CENTER

The Jefferson School City Center was once a high school for African-American students in Charlottesville, established in 1926. Today, the building houses the African-American Heritage Center, a collection of historical exhibits and a center for education and special events. Visitors can attend lectures and enjoy concerts and films. A rich resource for those interested in local history and genealogy is the Isabella Gibbons Local History Center on site at the Jefferson School, with an archive of more than 60 oral histories of students who attended the school between 1930 and 1960.

175 4th St. NW, 434-260-8720
jeffschoolheritagecenter.org

MEET A WRITER
AT THE VIRGINIA FESTIVAL OF THE BOOK

The Festival of the Book, a program of the Virginia Foundation for the Humanities, has something for all readers. The festival lasts five days and attracts readers and writers from all over the Commonwealth. Highlights include a business breakfast, keynoted by a well-known author; small sessions for aspiring crime-fiction writers, biographers, romance novelists and the like; and a kids' fair. Charlottesville is full of bookstores, writers, and readers, among them John Grisham, John Hart, Rita Mae Brown, Kathryn Erskine, and more . . . spot a famous writer at the festival, or hear one speak! Book signings abound, so bring your book allowance and be prepared to stock up.

Virginia Foundation for the Humanities
145 Ednam Dr., 434-924-3296
www.vabook.org/index.html

SEE THE LIGHTS OF KEY WEST
DURING THE HOLIDAYS

The Key West Neighborhood really lights it up for the holidays. Not only do the homeowners get on board with lights and inflatables, Griswold-style, and the neighbors line the streets with luminaria—you know, what used to be paper bags filled with sand and glowing with a lit candle inside. Nowadays, sometimes the bags are plastic and the lights electric, but the effect is the same (and safer). It's a beautiful sight to behold, particularly if we're lucky enough to score a white Christmas. Take a walk, not just a drive, through the neighborhood to get the full impact of the scene. Key West is located one mile north of Charlottesville on VA Route 20. Interesting history lesson: the land is the west side of the property granted to a man named Martin Key in 1731 by George II, King of England.

Key West Neighborhood Association
393 Key West Dr.
keywest.avenue.org

DIG UP A LITERARY TREASURE
AT THE UNIVERSITY OF VIRGINIA LIBRARY

Alderman Library at the University of Virginia boasts 5 million books and journals from around the world. With a Virginia resident ID you can check books out. If you're from elsewhere, you're welcome to read and research on-site.

If that's not enough to whet your bibliophile appetite, check in to the Albert and Shirley Small Special Collections Library. The Small Library features more than 16 million objects, including manuscripts, archival records, rare books, maps, broadsides, photographs, audio and video recordings, and more. It's a seriously cool exhibit for anyone with a love of literature and history.

Alderman Library

160 McCormick Rd., Charlottesville 22904
434-924-3026

Albert and Shirley Small Special Collections Library

P.O. Box 400110, Charlottesville 22904
434-243-1776
www.library.virginia.edu
small.library.virginia.edu
smallnotes.library.virginia.edu

BLESS THE HOUNDS
AT GRACE EPISCOPAL CHURCH

A very sweet, and very typically Charlottesville, tradition is more than 80 years old and takes place every Thanksgiving morning. The Blessing of the Hounds is a special gathering at Grace Episcopal Church in the community of Keswick. Since 1929, the church has cleverly enticed fox hunters to come to church on Thanksgiving morning, offering special blessings for their hunting dogs and horses. In the oldest ceremony of its kind in the United States, more than a thousand people come to witness the Keswick Hunt Club dogs receive their blessing. If you're a dog or horse lover and want a special way to kick off Thanksgiving, this is it.

5607 Gordonsville Rd., Keswick 22947
434-293-3549
www.gracekeswick.org

HONE YOUR CRAFT
AT WRITERHOUSE

WriterHouse is an unbelievably rich resource for the wannabe writer and those who have already published. WriterHouse is both location and organization, providing space for writers in which to work, undistracted, free from coffeehouse patrons or well-intentioned friends and family members. It's also a collection of programs and classes for all levels of writing expertise and various writing disciplines. In addition, it's a place where writers can gather and meet to help one another through critique groups, mentoring, readings, and other events. It's the place for writers; a home away from home and a room of one's own. Join, write, teach, learn, or just visit.

508 Dale Ave., 434-296-1922
www.writerhouse.org

FOLLOW THE H₂O
WITH RIVANNA WATER AND SEWER AUTHORITY

Do you know where your water comes from? Or what happens when you flush the toilet in Charlottesville or Albemarle County? If you care about conservation, or learning about the watershed and how to protect it for the immediate and long-term future, this educational adventure is right up your alley. The Rivanna Conservation Society offers guided school and public tours of the Rivanna Water and Sewer Authority's Moores Creek Wastewater Treatment Facility, where participants learn exactly where our award-winning, clean, safe, drinking water comes from and is processed for our consumption. The tours also highlight what happens to the wastewater produced by the many citizens of the region. Learn appreciation for the processes and planning that go into making sure our water resources are sustainable and what you can do to help conserve and recycle, contributing to the overall health of our community.

Rivanna Conservation Society
108 5th St. SE #206, 434-977-4837
www.rivannariver.org
www.rivanna.org/home.htm

TOUR SWANNANOA PALACE

Swannanoa Palace is a sight to behold. A 1912 Italian-inspired marble masterpiece unexpectedly rises atop Afton Mountain against the backdrop of Nelson County in central Virginia. The 52-room marble palace was built by Major James Dooley, a Richmond railroad executive, as a tribute to his beloved wife. It is a replica of the Villa Medici in Rome, created by more than 300 artisans at the bargain price of just $2 million. There's an elegant palace garden, a 4,000-piece Tiffany stained-glass window, and a domed ceiling with Mrs. Dooley's likeness. It's something else to see! There are limited weekend visiting hours, and while children are welcome, Swannanoa is definitely an attraction more of interest to grownups.

497 Swannanoa Lane, Afton 22920
540-942-5201
www.virginia.org/Listings/HistoricSites/SwannanoaPalace

APPRECIATE ART
AT THE MCGUFFEY SCHOOL

The McGuffey School was built in 1916 and in 1975 was reborn as an art center. Classrooms were converted into airy, spacious art studios, and three galleries provide the largest art display space in Charlottesville. More than 45 artists rent space at McGuffey, but the organization has well over 150 members who display art in the galleries and participate in events. Every first Friday of the month is a new gallery opening, and when the art center is open, so is the gift shop, so you can take home your own piece of locally created art.

201 2nd St. NW, 434-295-7973
mcguffeyartcenter.com

SPOOK YOURSELF
ON THE SPIRIT WALK GHOST TOUR

The Spirit Walk Ghost Tour is held in late October and is the main fund-raiser for the Albemarle Charlottesville Historical Society. There's a Maplewood Cemetery Tour and a Court Square Tour, both with hair-raising history lessons.

Albemarle Charlottesville Historical Society
200 2nd St. NE, 434-296-1492
www.albemarlehistory.org

TIP
History isn't limited to the center stage for Halloween. The Historical Society offers one-hour walking tours of Court Square each Saturday at 10 a.m. and every Thursday at 5:30 p.m.

VISIT THREE PRESIDENTS' HOMES

Thomas Jefferson's Monticello gets all the attention. Don't skip out on seeing the other two presidents' homes in the region, however. A short distance away—in Orange, Virginia—Montpelier is the home of James Madison. The restored home of James and Dolley Madison is an interactive, educational experience, and the gardens are majestic to behold. The recent reconstruction of slave quarters, the work of more than two decades of archeology on the property, tell a more in-depth story of our nation's history. Highland, the home of James Monroe, is practically spitting distance from Monticello. You can earn serious historic street cred by touring all three.

James Madison's Montpelier

13384 Laundry Rd., Montpelier Station 22957
540-672-2728
www.montpelier.org

James Monroe's Highland

2050 James Monroe Parkway, Charlottesville 22902
434-293-8000
ashlawnhighland.org

Thomas Jefferson's Monticello

931 Thomas Jefferson Parkway, Charlottesville 22902
434-984-9800
www.monticello.org

CELEBRATE OUR FOUNDERS
WITH THE TOMTOM FOUNDERS FESTIVAL

Twice a year, this crowd-sourced community festival pops up seemingly out of nowhere and pulls off a plethora of events all over town. Once in April and once in October, the TomTom Founders Festival schedules concerts, block parties, talks on innovation, business in our community, entrepreneurial pitch competitions, and creative expos.

www.tomtomfest.com

PLAY INDOORS
AT VIRGINIA DISCOVERY MUSEUM

An indoor playland with hours of learning disguised as fun, the Virginia Discovery Museum is a great experience for little people. A pint-sized C'ville has a restaurant, a post office, and a theatre to inspire hours of pretend play. The Discovery Museum encourages family play, so no break for mom and dad—get down on the floor and play right along with the young ones.

524 E. Main St., 434-977-1025
www.vadm.org

BE LOCALLY, SOCIALLY AWARE

In the summer of 2017, Charlottesville was the site of the largest-to-date recorded gathering of white supremacists. Heather Heyer, an anti-racism activist, was killed when a white nationalist rally participant drove his car into the crowd, injuring many others. Fourth Street NE, the site of the tragedy, has been renamed with signage declaring it Heather Heyer Way. The section of sidewalk often has chalk drawings, flowers, candles, and other mementos honoring Heather. Stop by, pay your respects, and think about the role racism plays not just in Charlottesville, but in our country, and what we can do to affect change. As Heather said in her final Facebook post before her death, "If you're not outraged, you're not paying attention."

If you're a local resident, get involved in area nonprofits, join a committee, get to know your neighbors, or run for local office.

SEE A TRULY SPECTACULAR TREE
ON THE GROUNDS AT UVA

You might think that seeing one particular tree wouldn't make a list of this kind, but this isn't just any tree. Found on the west side of the Rotunda on UVA's Grounds, this Gingko tree was planted in 1860 by UVA's first superintendent, William Pratt. Known as the "Pratt Gingko," this majestic tree turns color late in fall, then drops its leaves practically all at once, carpeting the ground beneath with golden leaves. It is the universal sign, at the university, that winter has come.

VIEW AN ABORIGINAL ART COLLECTION

The Kluge-Ruhe Aboriginal Art Collection of the University of Virginia is the only museum in the United States dedicated to the exhibition and study of Australian Aboriginal art. The museum features the art and culture of Australia's indigenous people.

The Kluge-Ruhe Collection opened in 1997 through a gift by Charlottesville businessman John W. Kluge (1914–2010). In the late 1980s and 1990s, Kluge compiled one of the finest private collections of Australian Aboriginal art in the world.

The collection includes acrylic paintings, blown glass, installations, drawings, photographs, and more. It's the only collection of its kind, and it's right here in Charlottesville.

Kluge-Ruhe Aboriginal Art Collection
400 Worrell Dr., 434-244-0243
www.kluge-ruhe.org

STARGAZE
AT MCCORMICK OBSERVATORY

On Friday nights, the McCormick Observatory at the University of Virginia Department of Astronomy opens to the public. Get a chance to observe the stars and planets through the McCormick and Fan Mountain telescopes. Weather permitting—clouds tend to get in the way of stargazing—guests are invited to peek at the sky through all the facility's telescopes and experience audio-visual presentations, museum exhibits, and tours of the observatory. Faculty, post-doctoral candidates, and graduate students host and answer questions. It's a great outing for a group, date, or family night. Call ahead.

600 McCormick Rd., 434-924-7494
www.astro.virginia.edu

GO TRICK-OR-TREATING
ON THE LAWN AT UVA

Easily the cutest sight of the year, children are invited to Trick or Treat at the University of Virginia at the 54 student rooms that line the Lawn (and are traditionally awarded as residences to top students). More than 70 student-run organizations donate candy to be dispensed to cherubs in costume. The event happens every Halloween from 4 p.m. to 6 p.m. and is a great defined way to safely usher young children through their first door-to-door Halloween experience. For parents, it's a delightful way to see the community in costume and hobnob with friends while little ones play and collect their goodies. It's a pretty great town-plus-gown event and a nice way to spend some time on the Grounds as a guest.

GIVE YOUR TIME AND TALENT
TO AN AREA NONPROFIT

In the aftermath of the events of August 12, 2017, Charlottesville had an influx of donor attention from the rest of the country. Nonprofits that serve the local population do so by helping the homeless with shelter, feeding the hungry, providing affordable housing assistance, and much more. Volunteer opportunities abound. Skilled construction volunteers are needed for Building Goodness Foundation's local efforts to improve the facilities of nonprofit partners. Tutors are needed with Literacy Volunteers to help adults for whom English is a second language improve their reading skills. Cooks and servers are needed to help PACEM with overnight stays of homeless folks through the winter months, and at The Haven, our day shelter. Volunteer time is a year-round need in Charlottesville

Building Goodness Foundation
Literacy Volunteers of Charlottesville/Albemarle
PACEM
The Haven

SHOPPING AND FASHION

TO MARKET, TO MARKET
AT THE CITY FARMERS' MARKET

Spend any Saturday morning—April through December—at the City Market, an open air festival of fresh, local produce and handcrafted items; and dairy, eggs, and meat from animals raised just a few miles away, responsibly and organically. While you're strolling and people-watching, visit the best authentic Mexican taco stand you'll ever find (the line is worth it), or eat a doughnut fresh from the fryer while sipping a fresh-brewed cup of coffee made with locally roasted beans. Most vendors are cash-only, but the City Market offers credit or debit purchase of tokens that can be used in place of cash with all vendors. Leave your pets at home (sorry, they're not invited), wear comfortable shoes, and plan to see plenty of people you know, and many you don't, any Saturday at the City Market.

207 First St. S., 434-970-3371
www.charlottesvillecitymarket.com

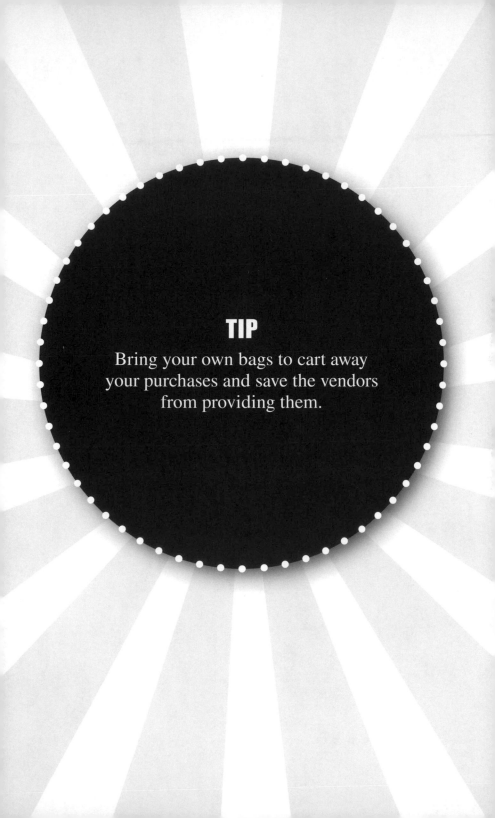

TIP

Bring your own bags to cart away
your purchases and save the vendors
from providing them.

FIND GREAT JUNK
AT AN ECLECTIC RESALE SHOP

In college, my friend Ellen was fond of "going junking," the term she applied to long Saturdays exploring consignment and used goods stores. These abound in the Commonwealth, from the upscale to the rare antique collection to the battered, truly used yard sale "junk." There are treasures out there for anyone. Some favorite stops for eclectic shopping are listed on the next page.

Circa

1700 Allied St., Charlottesville 22903
434-295-5760
www.circainc.com

Low

105 Fifth Street SE, Charlottesville 22902
434-293-8092

The Habitat Store

1221 Harris St., Charlottesville 22903
434-293-6331
www.cvillehabitat.org/about-store

The CASPCA Rummage Store

943 Preston Ave., Charlottesville 22903
434-293-8475
caspca.org/rummage-store

GET CUSTOM THREADS
AT ALTON LANE

It's an experience like no other: you book an appointment, arrive at a beautifully appointed showroom, and sip fine bourbons while undergoing a 3-D body scan. Then, you select from a plethora of styles, fabrics, and other custom options that will make you feel like you've both gone back in time and traveled to the future simultaneously. For dudes only (but ladies are welcome to accompany their guys and offer opinions), Alton Lane specializes in bespoke suits, shirts, and perfect fit. The Downtown Mall showroom is available by appointment only. Delivery of custom made shirts is around 16 days; suits take approximately four weeks.

Alton Lane
112 Fourth Street NE, 888-800-8616
www.altonlane.com

EAT FROM A TREE
WHILE YOU SHOP AT EDIBLE LANDSCAPING

Edible Landscaping is not merely a landscaping store; rather, it's a Garden of Eden on the outskirts of Charlottesville. Wander the rows of fragrant flowering fruit trees and explore varieties of plants and shrubs you've never considered. Learn what grows well in this climate and what you shouldn't bother planting. Don't eat lunch before you go in the summertime; instead, stroll around sampling blueberries, strawberries, apples, and peaches from their source. You'll be entranced and, if you're not already, convinced that you, too, can be a farmer. Come to learn and to buy; prepare to be enchanted.

361 Spirit Ridge Lane, Afton 22920
434-361-9134
www.ediblelandscaping.com

TURN A PAGE
AT AN INDEPENDENT BOOK STORE

Virginia may be for lovers (as the tourism slogan tells us), but Charlottesville is for readers. E-books and big box bookstores seem not to have hurt the book trade, both new and pre-owned, throughout the Charlottesville region. Pore over rare reading treats in a variety of environments, from the very well-lit and organized—New Dominion opened its doors in 1924 and is local author John Grisham's store of choice for book launches and signings—to the floor-to-ceiling, basement labyrinth experience that is Daedalus Bookshop. Browse carts and shelves of used books for gifts or your personal collection. I promise you'll find something you or someone you know will want to read.

New Dominion

404 E. Main St., Charlottesville 22902
434-295-2552
www.newdominionbookshop.com

Oakley's Gently Used Books

112 W. Main St. #9, Charlottesville 22902
434-977-3313
www.oakleysusedbooks.com

Daedalus Bookshop

121 4th St. NE, Charlottesville 22902
434-293-7595

Blue Whale Books

115 W. Main St., Charlottesville 22902
434-296-4646
www.bluewhalebooks.com

Read It Again Sam

214 E. Main St., Charlottesville 22902
434-977-9844

STROLL FIELDS
OF LAVENDER
AT WHITE OAK LAVENDER FARM

In nearby Rockingham County, be transported to a field in France, or at least in your imagination. At White Oak Lavender Farm, more than 8,000 plants in many varieties make for some pretty spectacular scenery and photo opportunities. Shop for lavender-infused products in the shop, or take a workshop and learn to make a lavender wreath, sachets, and eye pillows, or how to grow your own lavender plants. Wine tasting at the on-site Purple Wolf Vineyard begins at noon daily.

2644 Cross Keys Road., Harrisonburg
540-421-6345
www.whiteoaklavender.com

PAINT A PLATE
AT LAZY DAISY

A great rainy-day activity, or a good group playdate for kids *or* grownups, painting pottery is fun, relaxing, and occasionally productive! Since the shop opened, friends have been crafting an eclectic collection of dessert plates, made two at a time, no two the same. Kids love the creativity involved in choosing a pottery piece; selecting stencils, colors, and other tools; and painting away with no lines or rules. Good for birthday parties or just a solo project, Lazy Daisy is an easy way to get handcrafted pottery you paint yourself.

1709 Monticello Rd., 434-295-7801
lazydaisyceramics.com

SHOP 'TIL YOU DROP
AT BARRACKS ROAD

The town's best collection of chain stores and boutiques is the Barracks Road Shopping Center. This is the spot for serious wardrobe enhancement and retail therapy. Choices range from a high-end shoe and accessory boutique to Old Navy, Michael's Arts and Crafts, Banana Republic, Chico's, J. Jill, Anthropologie, and Ann Taylor Loft, to name just a few. Strategically placed restaurants make it possible to spend a long day of shopping with breaks for sustenance.

1117 Emmet St. N., 434-977-0100
www.barracksroad.com

PAINT AND SIP
WITH GUIDED INSTRUCTION

Take an instructor-guided painting class, completing a project in a relaxed social setting, sipping wine, and applying color to canvas. Go alone and meet other artists, with a friend or a group, or book the entire class for a private party. Most classes have a singular focus: a defined project like painting a seasonal scene, a still-life, or a local landmark. If the more you drink, the better you paint, this is the experience for you.

Wine and Design
609 E. Market St., 434-218-3112
www.wineanddesignus.com/location/charlottesville-va/home

Muse Paintbar
2050 Bond St #110, 434-829-3060
www.musepaintbar.com/events/charlottesville-paint-bar

SHOP FOR A CAUSE
AT MARTHA'S MARKET

Martha's Market features an excellent collection of vendor exhibitors from all over the country gathered for a single weekend under the roof of the John Paul Jones Arena. You pay a fee to shop this carefully curated collection, and it's all for a cause. Martha's Market, an annual event put on by the Martha Jefferson Hospital's Women's Committee to raise money for women's health, features more than 70 unique boutiques with wares you won't find anywhere else. The Women's Committee has been successful in raising more than $4 million for outreach to women in underserved populations in areas like breast health, midlife health, and heart disease.

John Paul Jones Arena
295 Massie Rd., 888-575-8497
www.mjhfoundation.org

SUGGESTED
ITINERARIES

MUSIC LOVERS

DATE NIGHT

SPORTS FANS

• •

FESTIVALS

THE GREAT OUTDOORS

FOODIE FAVORITES

• •

JUST OUT OF TOWN

FUN WITH KIDS

OFF THE BEATEN PATH

ACTIVITIES
BY SEASON

There's always fun to be had in Charlottesville, but some events and activities are best enjoyed, or only happen, at specific times of year. Here are some ideas to keep you busy no matter the season:

WINTER

SPRING

SUMMER

FALL

INDEX

• •